How Can I Serve You?

A Fresh Perspective for Youth Leaders to Nurture Teens

Virginia S. Rector, MCRP, MA, MTS

Foreword by:
Rev. Dr. Lonnie E. Rector

BK Royston Publishing
P. O. Box 4321
Jeffersonville, IN 47131
502-802-5385
http://www.bkroystonpublishing.com
bkroystonpublishing@gmail.com

© Copyright – 2018

All Rights Reserved. No part of this book may be reproduced, stored in a retrieval system, or transmitted by any means without the written permission of the author.

Cover Photo Credit: Wanda Woods, "Wheat/Die to Self" John 12:24

Additional Photo Illustration: Derrick Thomas

Cover Textual Graphics: Brent Barnett

ISBN-13: 978-1-946111-65-4

Printed in the United States of America

Dedication

This guide is dedicated to Pop Pop and GiGi's grandsons Sebastian and Shane. They have great influence over our family. We pray for God to continue to cover, lead, guide and protect them while we hold them close as God is preparing them for what they shall be.

Let us be mindful that we must take advantage of the seasons of influence we currently have. We must build into the lives of those God brings across our path today (leadlikejesus.com).

Be very careful, then, how you live—not as unwise but as wise, making the most of every opportunity, because the days are evil. — Ephesians 5:15-16

Acknowledgements

I thank God for the persons who were instrumental in my husband and me attending the 84th Celebration of the National Convention of Gospel Choirs and Choruses held in Baltimore, MD in 2017. It was our first time attending the convention, and it is where I met Julia and Brian Royston. While participating in her eBook writing session, she forged my confidence to a new level. I am grateful to BK Royston Publishing for the coaching that followed, which led to publishing this guide. Her words, "Keep Writing" and "Let's Go!" were exhilarating. She didn't know me, or my ability, yet she expected me to write. She inspired me more than she will ever know. I want to thank the individuals who will read this guide and I hope it will be a blessing to them. I am not suggesting this reading as a cure to all that may be encountered. In fact, there are many other guides that exist. On the other hand, I am confident that this is a divinely inspired perspective that should be read and applied.

Thank you to my loving husband who demonstrated patience as I entered into days and late nights of deep thought and processing. I'd like to thank Dr. Gloria Boozer whose persuasion of research and copious documentation allowed me to assist her as she created an updated history book published for the Epsilon Beta Omega Chapter and included the chartering of the undergraduate Rho Tau Chapter of Alpha Kappa Alpha Sorority, Inc. at the University of South Carolina Spartanburg. I must thank Dr. Nancy Fox for inviting me to write the Forward in the Lyme Disease Curriculum she authored. Soon thereafter, she observed in 2015 that I should include a chapter in her book, Decisive Women, which provided me with another opportunity to be published. I want to thank the English, History, teacher friends and administrators from Elkton High School including Ms. Avery, Ms. Porcelli, Mr. Brizell and Ms. Lamb's 9th grade class anthology of essays, "Behind the Doors of G110" for further inspiring me to write. Special thanks to Ms.

Alison McLean for her nurturing spirit. Also, to the very talented teachers and staff at Hodgson Vocational Technical High School for demonstrating how beneficial it is to not only teach, but to learn from youth. To Dr. Wynand deKock, thank you for taking off our "training wheels" during Open Seminary, compelling students to dig a little deeper when searching for theological meaning and applying God's Word. Thank you to Dr. K for over 20 years of allowing me to mentor you and now, we mentor each other. To Dr. Sarah Simmons, thank you for including me in your dissertation. I am very appreciative of the space and time that Stellar award winner Bro. Alphaeus Anderson has provided with training youth at my church, as well as, creatively disseminating excellent information through workshops with youth, mentors and leaders across the U.S. and abroad. I also recommend reading his step-by-step guide, *Youth Magnet*. I am so grateful for the role modeling, dedication, time, and care Dr. Melanie Thomas Price administers to develop children and to support parents. To Raenita Shazier, along with the Continental Society-Delaware Chapter, Inc., thank you for the volunteer services rendered to encourage youth to reach their greatest potential. I would be remiss if I didn't thank all youth leaders, ministries and advisors, and the Pilgrim Baptist Church family for always putting love, care, and service into action. To my close friends who unassumingly make infinite contributions behind the scenes, you are priceless. Also, thank you to my family for your willingness to always listen and share your input. You are a blessing to me. Youth Leaders, in the mist of serving teens let's continue to move forward by applying the following, "When Jesus Christ asked little children to come to him, he didn't say only rich children, or White children, or children with two-parent families, or children who didn't have a mental or physical handicap. He said, let all children come unto me." Marian Wright Edelman

Table of Contents

Dedication	iii
Acknowledgements	v
Foreword	xiii
Growth is a Process	1
Background and Foundation	1
Introduction	4
What Does Becoming A Youth Leader Entail	16
Why Is Healthy Parental (Guardianship) Involvement Needed	21
Establishing A Budget	29
Organic Realities	33
Meeting the Need of Teens: Understanding Culture, Climate, and Norms	33
A. Helping Teens to Understand What Love Is	48
B. Teens Believe Distractions Are Supposed to Happen	49
Integration of Social Media	61
Questionnaire: How are Teens Responding	66
Doing Something	81

How Will the Church Respond: How Can Ministries Collaborate?	81
Formation and Transformation	89
Community Partnerships	97
Conclusion	100
Epilogue	105
References	107
Teen Icebreakers and Activities	**111**
Finding My Purpose and Activities	111
What Makes Me Happy?	113
Being Alone With God Is A Good Thing; Be Sure You Are Spending Some Time With HIM!	115
Challenging Myself, Setting New Goals: Doing Something Different	117
Out Of My Hands	119
Peers Acting Like Alligators	121
Believe It Or Not, Adults Can Learn Some Valuable Lessons From Youth	123
Notes	**125**

Foreword

There is never a dull moment with my wife of thirty-four years. Virginia Rector has had a heart for working with youth since she was a young girl. If you had a conversation with her, she would share that she was an imperfect teenager. On the other hand, she recognizes that some of the hard-core lessons she learned while growing up were not as bad as she thought. In fact, those lessons taught her to become a godly woman, a dedicated wife and an awesome mother, mother-in-law and grandmother. Virginia is an emerging author who believes that while growing into Christ-likeness, becoming saturated with the fruit of the spirit is essential.

She and I appreciate the opportunity rendered by Julia Royston to be mentored, which allowed this guide to be published. From living in South Carolina to Delaware, Virginia has been gifted to chronicle her own story, including parallels and blends of values practiced by others who understand the transformational challenges that adolescents face. It is her deepest desire that readers will view this resource as a different perspective to guide emerging Youth Leaders, as they help teens to seek a relationship with Jesus Christ. It is our hope that persons involved with youth will gain some new insights as to how to work patiently with those who will someday replace us. With that endeavor, there is just one request I have for all born again believers in Christ. Before forging ahead, "first, pray." Some will say that's a redundant cliché, but talk to God, have a conversation with Him, communicate with Him, pray about it; prayer still works.

Lovingly Your Husband,

Lonnie

Reverend Dr. Lonnie E. Rector

HOW CAN I SERVE YOU?

How Can I Serve You?

Growth is a Process

Background and Foundation

The iGeneration, also known as Generation Z, the technology or digital generation or the post millennial generation, to name a few refers to youth born during the year of 1994 or later who has accepted use of technology as an extension of themselves and often as a substitute for direct human interaction. According to a Harvard Business Review report, Bill Gates proposed that we call this next wave Generation I, for Internet. Gates described them as the first generation to grow up with the Internet.

With this in mind, it is important for youth leaders to recognize how interacting with young people has evolved; it is an act of *longsuffering*. While accepting the challenge of training them, understanding how to relate to the youth is the first step to inspiring them to look ahead and seek positive goals, accept guidance from knowledgeable resources and desire a brighter future.

As we use the scriptures for our basis to create a blueprint, Proverbs 22:6 says we are to, "Train up a child in the way he (she) should go and when he (she) is old he (she) will not depart from it." Too often, today's youth have to train themselves. Nationwide for child homelessness, Arizona ranks fifth worst state. Historically, Psalm 78:5 reminds us, "He decreed statutes for Jacob and established the law in Israel, which he commanded our forefathers to teach their children." Also, we are mandated by Titus 2, that the mature men and women are to teach the young. When we think of the story of how the eagle teaches its young eaglets to fly our mission becomes similar; in the process of adolescent growth, when our youth begin to fall, we must undergird them and take the lead. Given, we may be the only Bible some teens may read, there is a need for

How Can I Serve You?

a *"how-to"* guide, that demonstrates our ability to assist with their growth. It is sometimes difficult for youth to think of us as ever having been their age, therefore it is the intent of this guide to:

Look back at how we functioned as teens, describe the role of a youth leader, the need for healthy parental (or guardian) involvement and commitment, share the importance of establishing a budget, understanding the culture, climate and norm, and integration of social media, differentiate formation and transformation, and discuss how the church can offer support and provide examples of how to partner with the community.

It is my desire, that this perspective will serve the purpose of helping Youth Leaders to conceptualize not only the desire, but also the commitment of this calling. If you want to pursue this journey, first, pray. Then, read Hebrews

13:16 which reminds us that we must not forget to do good and share with others, it pleases God.

Introduction

Several years ago, there was a story that I heard for the first time expressed by Senator Maggie W. Glover from the book, The Eagles Who Thought They Were Chickens by Mychal Wynn. Senator Glover articulated the manner in which, a great eagle was captured, its wings were clipped and he was held captive in a yard with chickens where three eagle eggs layed. Fortunately, the eagle was secure in his self-image, culture and heritage. Although, when hatched they were laughed at; the mature eagle began to teach, encourage and coach the young eagles to realize their greatest potential to rise above low expectations oftentimes demeaning conditions.

How Can I Serve You?

Every teen, while growing-up should have some pleasant memories. I admit, I wasn't perfect, and I was reared with humble beginnings. My memories as a teen began at 686 Gregory Street, where our parents offered a warm and friendly environment. We resided on property where my father and his siblings once lived. In fact, to keep the memory alive, one of my cousins, who now lives in Los Angeles, was named after our street. Youth were always around, these were fun times. Sounds of music, singing, and laughter filled the house; there was an atmosphere of *goodness*. It was a common practice for adults to ask the question, *who are your parents, who are your relatives, what church do you attend*? That's how neighbors measured the standards of an individual. There was always a place at the table for one more because our mother was a good cook and didn't mind sharing a meal. Visitors came by daily to sit awhile and have a cup of coffee. Cordiality kept children coming back again and again. Neighbors were familiar and looked out for the youth. It was customary in the south for children to address adults with "yes ma'am and no sir." The pastor and schoolteacher were once notable people in the community. We all lived in the same neighborhood; then, things changed. Today, neighbors rarely know each other. Youth have a prerequisite that before an adult can "outwardly" gain their respect, they must first "like" them. Too many teens exhibit a contumacious demeanor. As classrooms transition, some of the most talented 21st century teachers will creatively design a lesson, perhaps to the beat of a rap song, teach during the day, and for extra income be an Uber driver at night. The teacher, once considered a great role model for youth, deals with disruptions and constant unsettled behaviors that consume the first ten to fifteen minutes of each day. They must use warm-ups to redirect focus so teens can learn. For example, to offer something familiar, a high school teacher, on occasion infuses a few minutes of listening, recording, and sometimes translates communication using teen slang to get the attention of her students and before moving on to a new topic. Then, after getting them to focus, she smoothly transitions into the lesson. A commonly used website for teen slang is "netsanity.net." More prep time alone is needed to identify creative innovative ways to captivate their attention and engage students.

In too many instances, public education has become strained and the challenge to educate is more intense. Statistically, by the time teens reach middle and high school the reading level drops. In a recent study, 36% of low-income African American children passed a standard reading assessment for the third grade. The same study revealed that only 39% of Hispanic children passed, while over 60% of Caucasian and Asian children each passed. Rather than have the assistance they require, teachers find themselves sprinting around the classroom to serve 25-30 students; without alarm, Yale research found that students with relatively low literacy achievement tend to have more behavioral and social problems in subsequent grades. A dilemma with future impact is that along with not being literate, more teens are citing that becoming a teacher is not a preferred career choice.

In my upbringing, we were a church-going family. My mother, sister, and I attended a Pentecostal church where sometimes there were large numbers of youth and other times there were only a few. Pastors who were assigned to our church with children or grandchildren tended to attract more children. My dad and brother attended a Baptist church. We felt fortunate to have friends from both denominations. Although the

How Can I Serve You?

Pentecostal church had stricter rules, my parents provided us with a pretty normal upbringing (i.e., backyard birthday parties supported by large numbers of neighborhood youth, going to the movies). At my church, there was always an opportunity for young people to be involved. We practiced Romans 12:6 which says, "We have different gifts according to the grace given us." Some of our training emphasized "public speaking." Youth were also encouraged to use their talents to sing and play instruments; skills that were once highly cultivated in school and church. We believed that it is wise to use the gifts that God has given and to nurture the talents that allow growth. I was mentored in various capacities from junior usher, youth choir, secretary of the Sunday School, to president of the Young People's Ministry, which met on fourth Sunday afternoons. The Young People's Ministry also met periodically with youth who attended within the district diocese from over half of the state. Some of our best times were at Joy Night services where we released a lot of energy and met new friends. We also attended a National Young People's Institute Convention. At an early age, I presented at the National Youth Congress. From this experience, the *joy* of the Lord became my strength.

During our local church youth ministry meetings, we would learn about church doctrine, protocol, and scripture. Unlike today, technology was not the norm. Fellowship and face-to-face socialization were highly anticipated. Some of our favorite activities included playing a Bible verse baseball game while learning about various promises in the scripture. There was a lot of one-on-one and small group interaction.

The city's department of Parks and Recreation allowed me in my tween years to be among a few other youth who volunteered to work at the Austin Street

How Can I Serve You?

Community playground where we were introduced to a variety of new games. In the summer, Southside, Highland, and the neighborhood referred to as 'back of da college' were hubs where youth had the pleasure of enjoying activities several years before we did. Children from our neighborhood, as well as, youth from other communities would dazzle the park with fun competitions, laughter, and nutritional treats. Our Youth Leader, a high school Physical Education Teacher; a member of Omega Psi Phi, was a big, tall man with lots of patience and personality who was highly respected. Our summers were full of excitement. There were no drive-by incidences and few fights. The parks kept us physically and cognitively involved; the interaction gave us a safe place to be. Beyond this all-inclusive opportunity, for some unforeseen reason, out of all of the fun we were having, I noticed that there were children in my own community who weren't coming to the park.

As I became acquainted with them, I learned they were brothers and sisters who were caring for one another while their mother worked. I also found that although some of them were old enough to go to school, they were not attending because they had not received vaccines that were required to enroll in school. Since quite a few of the youth in the community did not attend church regularly, I asked if they would like to attend a Bible School in my backyard, and they agreed. I realized that by having a Bible Study outdoors, participants could wear whatever they wanted. At twelve, I observed that oftentimes we should not wait for youth to come to us, but when possible, we must physically meet them where they are. In other words, compared to the freedom felt by youth being outside in the park, youth could attend the Bible Study outside and not necessarily behind walls. It never dawned on me that I wasn't old enough or didn't have a seminary degree to accomplish the task. I didn't even think of my actions as mission's work. I just wanted to make a difference in the lives of youth. As I reflected, Ms. Steadman and Ms. Cheek former district youth directors had patiently invested in my teen years, they had a heart for encouraging and mentoring youth.

    As Youth Leaders, an attribute teens desired in which they emulated was *kindness*. Looking back, I also understand that God calls us into leadership roles whenever He wants. Richard Smallwood directed his first choir at the age of 11, Yolanda Caraway became involved in politics at the age of 14, Rev. Dr. Martin Luther King, Jr. enrolled at Morehouse College at the age of fifteen, Aretha Franklin recorded her first record in her teens and there are many others.

Virginia S Rector, MCRP, MA, MTS

After graduating from high school, I attended college. Church had become such a natural part of my being that while I was away from home I always found a church to attend. Furthermore, whenever there was a Sunday I missed going, there was a void. As I reflect, learning to attend church and developing a relationship with Christ at an early age helped me. Unlike some of my buddies, who left home, after we attended the party the night before Sunday was a great day to sleep in and do nothing. I followed the scripture, Hebrews 10:25 which, encourages us not to forget to come together to regularly worship. I had a love for church, enjoyed going to church, fellowshipping with old friends, as well as meeting new ones. Church kept me balanced; it gave me structure. While away from my biological family it gave me a sense of extended family. As times have changed, I noticed that keeping youth motivated and committed to attending church has become a challenge. They do not see the benefits of regular church attendance or view its value as an extended family. We must be mindful that *Koinonia*, the act of the Christians coming together in fellowship among people who have similar beliefs will keep teens unified and connected. The church is strengthening for youth and it creates space for a community of believers regardless of age, ethnicity, race, or gender.

When I was growing up, parents gave instructions and we followed-through with very rare moments of pushback, or rebellion. Today, rebellious practices are common and seem to be ever emerging among teens. Fortunately, there are people who still want to lead youth. Along with the resources needed to lead, pray about it, and ask God to give you the desires of your heart.

Virginia S Rector, MCRP, MA, MTS

What Does Becoming a Youth Leader Entail?

One of the first criteria for working with teen youth is that you must enjoy being around them. If you don't have the patience, stamina, love, or commitment to spend quality time with teens, then becoming a youth leader is not your calling. The work of a Youth Leader calls for some flexibility and strategic, yet creative thinking, that is beyond our personal comfort. Note: informal conversations regarding your hobbies and interests may be garnered in the minds of those who are seeking to select individuals who qualify; in other words, you will be observed.

To your benefit, if you are asked to serve, expect a job description outlining your responsibilities and duties as a reasonable request. Your personal testimony should be one that can wholeheartedly support Proverbs 3:1-6, with emphasis on the fifth verse, "Trust in the Lord with all your heart and lean not on your own understanding." Always pray before making a decision and listen for a response from the Lord.

Before allowing adults to work with youth, a background check could be required; in fact, the day may come when this is a mandatory prerequisite in Christian environments, similar to the requirements of providing services to youth in public venues. After being chosen to become a Youth Leader, in order to be effective, training will be needed. Contact hours of mentoring may extend well beyond once a month meeting. A Youth Leader may be asked to provide support that is not included on the position description. In other words, you may be invited to a school play, football or basketball game, choral recital, birthday or graduation party, or some other activity in which a teen is involved. Youth Leaders also need to *have the heart of a servant*. Being a Youth Leader is not a sideline position, or just being upfront. *Faithfulness* and loyalty is expected on a consistent basis. Even simple tasks of setting-up and tearing-down, preparing refreshments, or doing the prep work for meetings and events does not rest on the laurels of one or two people. It is everyone's responsibility to roll up his or her sleeves and participate. Leadership requires a team effort. Even youth participants are not exempt from helping out. Working together builds character and a sense of responsibility.

Being positive is important. Put your best face on the outside. Your body language and nonverbal actions will eventually be modeled by the youth you lead. Don't carry a scornful disposition; as Youth Leader, there will be times constructive criticism is needed; it will make you stronger. Try to always share a smile. Even when a situation appears negative, find a lesson to be learned or a positive note to end on.

How Can I Serve You?

*Being a **YOU**th **LEAD**er* means you are the person in charge; "**You Lead**." You are the one ultimately responsible for the safety, well-being, learning opportunities, and setting the atmosphere for youth, even behind the scenes. Be observant and prepare to recruit and train others who share similar compassion to help you. Don't get it twisted, it's nice to be thought of as a buddy or friend but earning their respect as an authority is a priority. Also, in most cases, communication should not be limited to the Youth Leader and the teen; communication should also be with the parent or guardian.

Eventually, passing the torch and teaching youth how to become leaders is a major component. Include them in decision making and give them choices but be prepared to guide them in the right direction even when your final decision is not a popular one. Be organized and ready to begin meetings with an outline of what will happen during the time you are together. Also, just in case your original plan has to be postponed, be creative and have a Plan B that you can easily grasp, as well as follow.

Determine when *confidentiality* is needed. Youth will need mentoring and may desire to share information with you that they only want you to know. While building a relationship with them, you must prove to be trustworthy. Oftentimes, the information may be from previous occurrences or situations that are unique to their maturation; they may need a listening ear. Recall that you were once their age and when asked, take some time to answer with a reflective response. In most cases, identify a scripture, a poem, quote, or resource that can help. On the other hand, when information shared is life-threatening being aware when it is time to share with the parent/guardian, pastor, or when to make another referral is critical. Do not allow yourself to be placed in a compromising situation. Making the wrong decision could jeopardize your future as a Youth Leader. Pray, and put on the whole armor of God, Ephesians 6:10-18, so that you may be able to stand against the schemes of the devil.

Why Is Healthy Parental (Guardianship) Involvement Needed

Parent participants with commitment to teens help their child to feel that the things in which they are involved is respected. Parental commitment also offers an opportunity for parents to create a support group for teens to get involved in activities such as chaperoning, fundraising, or to gain an observation of what the organization offers by volunteering. Parents can also recruit other parents to get involved and serve as a teen group advocate. The child feels valued when parents accept invitations to participate in an event or an activity alongside them. Share from a biblical perspective, that according to the ten commandments, having a supportive relationship with a parent has benefits of longevity whereby Ephesians 6:2-3, the first commandment with promise says, "Honor your father and mother,...that it may be well with you and you may live long on the earth." Provide support to parents as first responders to detect pitfalls, such as issues of anxiety, as well as when their child is in need of exceptional attention or care. Be mindful that not much compares to the love and support that is given by a parent.

    A little over thirty years ago, I became the wife of a pastor. Early on, I had a few seasoned pastors' wives who cared enough to be wonderful mentors. Working in ministry with my husband has afford some wonderful opportunities that brings to fruition the ever-evolving role of Youth Leader. I have facilitated a workshop on "intergenerational ministry," I teach Vacation Bible School and have served for about ten years as advisor/mentor to a 13-17-year-old teen girl's ministry. With the support of a compassionate music ministry consultant who has agape love for youth, I also offered a gospel music workshop and authored a step-by-step guide for mentors, teachers, parents, churches, and community organizations. Through these experiences, I learned more about how to work with teens. Some of the best advice I was given prior to accepting the teen ministry assignment was to get the parents involved. After all, that made sense because when the girls first join the ministry, they do not have a license to drive. A rewarding experience is, as the girls become older and transition to another level, they return to spend time and offer advice that is appreciated by the new teen girls who join the ministry.

Unfortunately, today there are times when the influence of parents may not provide desirable outcomes.

For instance, in *The Effects of Bad Parenting on Children*, a 2011 study conducted by the Joseph Rowntree Foundation with the UK Department of Education, found that teens exposed to inconsistent and harsh parenting, maternal depression and domestic violence may have antisocial tendencies. Parental drug overdose from opioids, which too often causes death, is also being witnessed by youth. Teen suicide, unfortunately, occur regardless of race, gender, or socioeconomic status. The study found that if teens haven't been taught coping skills, they might lack resilience, which can lead to depression. According to the study, these children are also two times more likely to misbehave (Richards-Gustafson, 2017).

Teen years, adolescence, is a formative age; among other things teens are dealing with gender identification and building self-esteem. The article, *Parental Divorce and Adolescents* states that when the adolescent is in a more disaffected and rebellious stage with parents, divorce can cause their grievances to intensify. In other words, rather than clinging to their parents, they pull away and become more independent from their family. Further, the impact of divorce is that teens often times will feel angry and less communicative, as well as, betrayed by broken parental commitment. Mentoring by Youth Leaders recurrently becomes a new source of trust and comfort for them.

There are also cases of children having to assume adult responsibilities before their time. A ten-year Special Educator, Scott Rector says, "Although, they're still young, oftentimes when teens have adult responsibilities they have a hard-time accepting instruction from an adult because at home, they are the adult." He has further observed that students who speak English as a second language will put on their "serious face" when dealing with individuals such as bill collectors or during school visitations when having to translate conversations for their parents with teachers and administrators. From these observations, the question sometimes entered our minds, "when did teens begin to gain authority equal to their parents?" An advantage to them assuming certain responsibilities early on is so that teens will gain an appreciation for the hard work that goes into acquiring funds to pay bills, and how to transact business affairs of the household. The downside can be when some teens begin to feel entitled; he or she believes some type of compensation is owed for every deed or accomplishment. For example, a teen who commented he was far too busy with academics and extracurricular activities to continue being involved in the youth choir but added that if he were chosen to become president of the choir, he would continue to be involved. Another concern is that when parents become elderly they seem to fear that their teen, may one day be their only source of love and care, therefore they are hesitant to asserting authority. According to U.S. News and World Report about 1.4 million children between ages 8 and 18 are caregivers nationwide (Esposito, 2015). However, should parents be held hostage by these statistics?

Bernita Cohen, a United States Air Force Veteran, shared that while working at a teen residential facility in Alaska, she received positive responses from teens when they felt that someone cared. She added that although they said they didn't want people telling them what to do, most teens during adolescence prefer some form of structure. Too often teens face a mountain of disappointments; in fact, there are so many, in order to stay above board, they may have to search for a shred of motivation from within. We must pray and encourage them from the scriptures as Psalm 71:5, says, "You are my hope; Oh Lord God, you are my confidence from my youth." Demonstrating self-control while working with teens can be an attribute they desire to see in an adult but is not necessarily practiced at home.

Reflect and share ways parents can be encouraged to be in involved in the lives of their teens:

_____

_____

_____

_____

_____

_____

_____

_____

_____

How Can I Serve You?

Establishing A Budget

The work accomplished by Youth Leaders requires a budget. Before creating a budget, you and your team should be in prayer and agree on what you want to do, why you want to do it, the desired outcome and what it would cost. You should also think in terms of creating an operational budget, projected costs and fundraising. As written in Habakkuk 2:2 the Lord will give you a vision (for your budget) that should be written down and made clear. This will help to eliminate confusion and should be readily interpreted by whoever reviews it. Create your budget and place it on a spreadsheet in order to keep up with expenditures and balances. At some point, you may be held accountable, so keep good records of funds raised and spending. Although your teen ministry may not have grown this comprehensively, discussions on the cost for youth leadership trainings, retreats, workshops, speakers for teens, field trips, activities, food, supplies, transportation, gifts, awards, and celebrations should be considered. According to Titus 2:7 pray about being a leader who shows in all respects to be a model, of good works, and in all your teaching show integrity, dignity, and wholesome speech that is above reproach. Pray for abundant funding when addressing the needs of teens. There may be times when they cannot travel to be exposed to opportunities that will broaden their learning. You may need to bring opportunities to them. Remember, your budget is a vision that should be made clear.

How Can I Serve You?

Reflect and list some of the items you would like to include in a budget for the teens that you will work with:

_____

_____

_____

_____

_____

_____

_____

_____

_____

_____

_____

_____

How Can I Serve You?

Organic Realities

Meeting the Need: Understanding the Culture, Climate and Norms

When I was a teen, eating meals together was traditional among families. Today, it is rare to hear a teen talk about sitting at home eating a meal together. The community youth were encouraged by parents to play outdoor games. We enjoyed riding our bikes up and down the street, roller skating, playing dodgeball, and red light/green light. We would play for hours, take a break to go home, eat, and then go back outdoors and play some more until the streetlights came on. In fact, rather than spending hours watching TV or video game screening, staying in the house around adult conversations, or running in and out of the house, parents would insist that we go outside and play, "get some fresh air." When we visited friends, our mother would advise us as to how long we should stay, we thought she was a little overprotective. It never crossed our minds that we could be shot while simply walking home. If we stayed beyond the designated time, she would either come and get us or call for us to return home. In our community, there were a couple of events designed for youth and we looked forward to participating in them annually. In the spirit of I Thessalonians 5:11, our mentors enjoyed having the opportunity to build us up. The first, although less than 35 miles from home, was considered to be a field trip. It was our Sunday School outing. Since most of our families didn't own a car, we would travel to Shelby, NC, on a school bus owned by a local African American mortician. The trip was to a park that had an indoor skating rink. A group of us who were younger would stand on the side to watch the teens have fun skating hand-in-hand. One of the teen couples, we admired, EJ and DJ later married. EJ and his siblings relocated to our hometown from Pittsburgh, PA; his dad was our pastor. During that time, rather than warring against teens, we were excited and embraced new youth who came to our church. We were anxious to stay actively engaged in various youth activities and singing was one of our favorites. EJ was a melodious vocal talent and had great influence with youth. One day, my mother and Ms. Steadman walked throughout the neighborhood to find him and asked if he would be choir director to lead about 30 youth in our church; they envisioned him as a great Youth Leader. He agreed and with his leadership, we sang gospel songs, and traveled throughout Georgia, South Carolina, and North Carolina. EJ also found time to play sports with the boys in the choir. Additionally, EJ along with his wife and a few other adults, chaperoned the choir on a trip to Myrtle Beach. He was an approachable, phenomenal Youth Leader. There was also great support from parents and the community which provided cookouts and fundraisers to help with transportation and uniforms. There are adults, who still have a passion for teens to be successful by dedicating time and resources towards positive experiences for them. During the summer, a former Delaware educator and his wife benevolently sponsor an academic camp for boys at a Historically Black University. Their hope is that the opportunity will help them to move forward in life.

Youth leaders must envision potential for individuals in the future to lead. Just as Paul entreated Timothy and Titus, similarly while adults are observing youth, youth are watching adults. Another activity located within the neighborhood regarded as fun and entertaining was held at Thompson Street Baptist Church. The youth didn't refer to the church without mentioning the pastor; the names were inseparable. Also, at that time he too had teen children. Regardless of our socio-economic status

How Can I Serve You?

Thompson Street was where we were passionate about attending Vacation Bible School. It was a safe place. The pastor had a powerful presence. He was highly respected, and the VBS teachers treated us the same. We learned Biblical lessons, sang songs, created crafts out of popsicle sticks, played on the church's playground, and on Friday evening at the close of VBS, we ate hot "chili" dogs. No one owned a cell phone. Our socialization depended on having face-to-face conversations, and in most cases, the adults inspired young children and teens to have career goals.

What we observed and experienced left a pleasant imprint in our minds? Today, youth are on their cell phone seven and eight hours per day. According to a CNN report, 50% of teens who own cell phones feel addicted. This may have an adverse effect on their social skills or self-image. Furthermore, when things with teens go awry, parents are asking the question, "where did we go wrong?"

Unfortunately, if teens don't get involved in a church that includes a focus on youth at an early age, oftentimes inappropriate behavior will become an inappropriate attribute that will follow them wherever they go (i.e., church, school, at their home or the home of a peer, events/activities, eateries and other social outings).

Most recently, during the summer, the Sewing and Sunday School ministries collaborated at my church to provide a week-long "Sewing Camp for Teens." The overall purpose was to increase the number of teens attending VBS. The seasoned women in the church who enjoy sewing assisted twenty-two teen girls and boys in making pajama bottoms, a fashion that teens found convenient to wear. While sewing is a life skill that appears to be dying, it provided an opportunity for an intergenerational ministry interactive activity. During a period of five days, lunch, career exploration, and games were offered. Initially, the camp served to be a pilot project that offered teens a viable skill, as well as, rekindled their interest in attending Vacation Bible School. The camp was a success and, in most cases, after sewing, teens would stay for two additional hours to attend VBS where they received another snack. These activities provided a safe place, a light meal, offered appropriate engagement, interaction with an older generation and an opportunity to learn and share a new skill. The teens also enjoyed being in harmony with their peers at a place where they could experience a daily time of fun, peace and learning. Proverbs 3:1-6 instructs us to train up a child in the way he (she) should go and when they become old, they will not depart from it.

Over three to four decades ago, teens wore mini dresses, bell-bottom jeans, platform heels, and Afros. Sly and the Family Stone transcended funk, rock, soul, and psychedelic music. Teens marched for civil rights and organized college sit-ins. Teens broke the barrier of, and integrated the Vietnam War. Youth who had just graduated from high school, integrated guerrilla warfare on the front lines of the Vietnam War. Places of worship were very segmented. Baptist were distinguished from Methodist and teens who worshipped at a Pentecostal church were called, "holy rollers." Youth rarely challenged the authority of their parents, teachers, preachers, and other adults. In the 60's youth in Birmingham, Alabama took the world stage when televised for the first time, standing in the gap for adults by marching and jailed for rising up against unfair practices of segregation. In the twenty first century, teen leaders in Florida have begun a "March for Our Lives" movement to stop gun violence, particularly in schools. During the developmental stages of adolescence, teens are attempting to answer the question, "Who am I?" As they determine their identity, they often seek their peers who are having the same experiences. They are seeking to make sense of values and social norms within society, but they may need guidance to find their purpose. The Apostle Timothy, from the scriptures was a teenager when he first met the Apostle Paul. It was through the influence of his beloved mother and grandmother that he became a believer of Jesus Christ. For teens who are striving to do what is right, 1 Timothy 4:12 serves as a reminder, "Don't let anyone look down on you because you are young, but set an example for the believers in speech, in conduct, in love, in faith and in purity." Leaders must nurture these attributes.

Teen group meetings in a church setting usually began with scripture and prayer. Don't be afraid to ask teens if they have a prayer request whether it is spoken or unspoken. They should know that they are not alone and that prayer is merely communicating with God. This practice is one they must be taught to rely on. As a consulting advisor to our teen girl's ministry, I initially asked the Lord to provide us with five girls. Each year, He either doubled or tripled the number requested to include teens from diverse backgrounds, ethnicities, and with special needs. For our team of advisors, it took us about three years to learn the type of workshops, trainings, field trips, and a variety of other events that would not only interest, but also keep the teens engaged. Teens are very observant and quick learners. We should not take for granted the limited amount of time we may have to help mold and shape them.

We also had to learn and understand how to connect to the mission and vision of church; this was made clear to the population within the teen girls' ministry we were asked to serve-- girls 13-17 years old. Also, we learned there would be a younger group of girls ages 8-12 who would later be referred to us when they became 13. This helped with our recruitment, but we also created a marketing plan to keep others aware of our presence and purpose. Some of our marketing strategies were as follows: We are described on the church webpage, and twice a year, the teens would create a newsletter that shared the activities the ministry had sponsored or collaborated with that would appeal to parents and teens. It is also important, to keep a record of permission forms that will need the signature of parents or guardians when offering special topics for discussion (i.e., human trafficking, teen domestic violence) and for activities like trampoline parks, and sleepovers. In this present age, we must be creative and engaging when brainstorming a variety of ways to be effective as we consistently teach and train youth. Transportation is one of a few areas where you may need to contract services or check with your church to determine what stipulations are covered by its insurance for transporting teens. Remember, before making transportation arrangements the need to have parents sign a permission form is imperative. The form should be designed to include the place and time of departure, time and location of the activity, who will be responsible for picking up the teen, medical history, and a phone number for who to contact in case of an emergency.

Some examples of life skills activities that we implemented were:

- college campus tours

- cultural and educational field trips

- career days

- service learning activities such as preparing and sending Christmas cards to deployed military service members

How Can I Serve You?

- serving breakfast and providing parent-relief at the Ronald McDonald House

Workshops (included, but were not limited to):

- parent workshops

- public speaking and managing finances

- the appropriate use of social media, included internet-based video games

- coordinating an annual sleepover with discussions on "self-image" and games

- a year-end gala celebration and reception

- a Teen Sewing Camp (offered during the week in conjunction with VBS)

- The girls also enjoyed going to the movies, therefore we made an effort to include a selection of movies that would provide a historical and self-image message content like *Hidden Figures*, as well as, on occasion a movie of their choice. We pray about the things that are planned, and as often as possible, incorporate a teachable moment into the time shared.

- Paint Party

- Bowling

- Hand Bell Ringing

- In conjunction with the youth department ministry, participation in "Hallelujah Night." (a safe place to be, an alternative to trick or treat which can include activities for the entire family)

How Can I Serve You?

Reflect and list some culture climate and norms you are aware of that are of interest to today's teens:

_____

_____

_____

_____

_____

_____

_____

_____

_____

_____

_____

_____

_____

Virginia S Rector, MCRP, MA, MTS

Helping Teens to Understand What Love Is

God is love. First, teens must be taught that when they see themselves in the mirror they see a person who is made in the image of God. As image bearers, we should teach them not to have a narcissistic demeanor, but to love themselves. A greater demonstration is for them to observe adults who love ourselves by how we treat our body (both internally and externally) as well as, how we serve others; hopefully, they will pattern after this behavior. Love is an action word. Romans 13:10 shares, "Love does no harm to a neighbor. Therefore, love is the fulfillment of the law." In order to be of value, we must share love with others. Pastor Joyce Meyers reminds us, "You cannot give away something you don't have in you." Love breeds from within and is displayed on the outside through our words and deeds. Teens need to observe that we are serious about our faith in Christ. Also, when teens move from their comfort zone and express themselves, they shouldn't feel they are going to be judged. It is imperative for us to understand there are times when listening may be the only and most important thing we need to do, at the moment. When we are asked for an explanation, it should be made simple and with clarity. The Holy Spirit should flow through us so that agape love becomes the light that shines and spreads to others.

Teens Believe Distractors are Supposed to Happen

Teen pregnancy is a distractor. During a September 28, 2017, NBC Evening News Report six decades ago, the word "pregnancy" could not be used on one of America's favorite television comedy shows, *I Love Lucy*. Moving forward in time, health stats reflect that teen mothers may birth babies that are preterm, or have low birth weight. A 2010 report by the Center for Disease Control states that pregnancy and birth are significant contributors to high school dropout rates among girls. It further reports that only about 50% of teen mothers receive a high school diploma by 22 years of age, whereas approximately 90% of women who do not give birth during adolescence graduate from high school. It also says that the children of teenage mothers are likely to be low achievers and to drop out of school, have more health problems, be incarcerated while they are an adolescent, and give birth as a teenager. Today, innocence seems to be almost non-existent; teens enjoy drama series like Teen Mom in the U.S. and Teen Mum in the UK. The Centers for Disease Control and Prevention recommends the implementation of evidenced-based teen pregnancy prevention programs, of which youth ministry can be placed under the category as both a youth development, and a community level program that addresses social and economic factors.

(www.cdc.gov/teenpregnancy/about/index.htm).

How Can I Serve You?

Drugs are a distractor. In 2010, national estimates indicated that approximately 6.2% of adolescents ages 12 to 17 have engaged in the nonmedical use of opioids. Because there is a dangerous black market, teenagers who are curious and susceptible can have easy access to drugs other than marijuana and vaping. Furthermore, teens who have been sexual victims, or traumatized by witnessing a violent act may become dependent on opioids such as fentanyl, Vicodin, OxyContin, Tylenol 3 with codeine, Percocet, Darvocet, morphine, methadone, buprenorphine, hydrocodone, oxycodone, and eventually heroin (Young, et. al., 2012). The overuse of drugs can be compared to the snake in Adam and Eve's experience while in the Garden of Eden, whereby teens are made to believe there is a "feel good experience they are enticed to try in which, without it they are convinced they would be missing a magical moment." Testimonials from previous drug abusers may help to redirect the behavior. Youth leaders, with the support of community-based organizations, can be upfront with incorporating a way to operationalize drug prevention vs. drug intervention trainings. Collaboration with a non-profit community-based drug awareness program may be ideal. Do some research, pray about it and God will direct you.

Bullying is a distractor. Teens, especially girls are often viewed as young drama queens. Adults may even think that observing dramatic behaviors among teen girls is both entertaining and cute. Actions that appear to be role playing can lead to distractions that have a negative impact on their lives. An excerpt from the guide, *The Teen Years Explained: A Guide to Healthy Adolescent Development* states that mood swings, trouble sleeping, inability to concentrate, avoiding classes, or not being social are classic behaviors of a victim of bullying. Recognition of these characteristics is critical during teen development. In fact, a 2001 national survey cited that 11% of students surveyed in grades 6 to 10 reported they had been bullied; these grades are inclusive of the ages that teen ministries serve. The report adds that bullying is more common among younger teens than older ones. Teens who are introvert, shy (quiet) may also become targets for bullying. According to the 2018 Kids Count Data Book, accidents, homicides and suicides in 2016 among teens ages 15 to 17 were 75% of deaths. A 2007 study shared that frequently bullied adolescents were five times more likely to have suicidal thoughts. The guide further warns that cyberbullying, a character-damaging form of bullying on the Internet, spreads quickly through the popular use of texting, instant messaging, and social networking. The study also found that the rate of girls participating in cyberbullying was 6% higher than boys. Youth Leaders can develop community partnerships to provide training on the appropriate use of technology and social media, cyberbullying and non-violent strategies to resolving disputes. Teen victims of bullying may begin to feel low self-worth, become withdrawn and isolated. In some cases, they may even develop the feeling that they need to carry a gun for protection (McNeeley, C. et. al., 2009). Pray about some of the negative decisions youth are making and that they will learn to look to God for an alternative.

Guns misused by teens are a distractor. While growing up, most of our neighbors knew each other. There was a community of pastors, teachers, church members, parents, relatives, and familiarity with whoever lived next door. As a teen, I can recall an older woman in our community who I used to refer to as "the nosey neighbor." Daily she would stand at her door as we got off the school bus. If a boy carried my books, before I got to the front door of our home, my mother was aware. If someone was shot, the entire community became alarmed. At the time, I didn't appreciate my neighbor's "snitching," but today with an increase in crimes against teens, we may need a few more individuals to speak-up. Today, teens playfully shoot each other with Roman candle guns that can leave serious wounds. Also, 3-D printed 'Ghost Guns' are accessible on the internet. There are present day examples of parents who work two and three jobs to provide for the needs of their household and children. Their hope is to make a better life for their child than what they had, but without extended family or supervision in place, youth will participate in inappropriate socialization. *Psychology Today* describes adolescence as years from ages 13-19 when teens are transitioning from childhood to adulthood and can begin as early as ages 9-12, depending on the child's maturity. Inherently, on September 9, 2017, a Delaware online news report headline read, *Wilmington: Most Dangerous Place in America for Youth.* The report stated that teens ages 12 and 17 will begin arguments on Twitter and Facebook and settle their disagreement by shooting one another. It further stated that the shootings were often related to "warring gangs." According to the report, persons who work with youth need not attempt to identify teens involved with warring gangs like in the 1980's, which was by wearing specific colors; teen gangs now use emojis and hashtags online. Mothers who were quoted in the report shared that they worked two jobs to meet the needs of their teens; and occasionally rewarded their child by carrying them on vacation trips of their choice. They were surprised to learn their teen had become involved in a gang for protection and friendship. They also had no idea where their parental communication with their child went wrong, as well as, how guns ended up in their home (Horn, et. al.,

2017). Distractions will come, but how teens respond can often determine the outcome.

Teens should be allowed to mature while participating in activities that are healthy and age-appropriate. Stronger personal connections and academic achievement occurs with teens who live in nurturing families and supportive communities. As Youth Leaders, we strive to help teens to develop a healthy and spiritual way of thinking which is grounded in the scripture. Proverbs 4:23 advises, "Above everything else, guard your heart for everything you do flows from it." Youth Leaders engage teens in Christian character-building workshops, hands-on activities, tutoring, cultural events, and most importantly introducing them to Jesus Christ, which will sustain their focus and redirect them toward productive and positive behavior. Dr. Melanie Thomas Price, CEO of Leap of Faith Child Development Center in Wilmington, DE, shared that

"Early learning is paramount, particularly among African American males residing in high poverty areas when entering school, in most cases, they are not ready." She passionately stated there are many factors that play a part in the breakdown of the family and community, however, the one element that stands out most for her is the parenting quality. In the child development center, Dr. Thomas-Price supervises 21 staff and serves up to 145 children. Kids Count, an Annie Casey Foundation 2011-2015 publication, reported over 95% of the children cared for reside with a single, low-income mother. The rate of single mother head of household in the Wilmington area is 53.8% and births to single African American mothers is 71.4%. With notable success, in an early-care and education setting, they have been providing learning and care for this population for 15 years. What was found is that many of the mothers are products of their environment. Dr. Thomas-Price believes that with the availability of parenting skills training, mentors, and opportunities for higher-level education, spiritual connections, and gainful employment we would witness a positive shift in our communities. Without assistance in these areas, we will continue to see violence, low self-esteem, and lack of hope in our neighborhoods. As the leader of the center, she humbly rolls up her sleeves and assumes the role of administrator, staff, and mentor to both teachers and young single mothers.

She added that she is proud yet concerned because she believes her center is doing a "good work," however, some of the societal trends are disturbing and heart wrenching. The high rate of violent crime perpetrated by teens and millennials in communities is skyrocketing. She stated that fostering stronger families is the key to safer neighborhoods, healthier cities, productive States, and in turn a greater America. She strongly advocates for Parenting Classes that prove to be helpful to families. "Many parents are simply lacking parenting skills and teens are out of control. We may not see immediate change, but the seed would have been planted." She is a firm believer in seed, time and harvest. Dr. Thomas-Price shared that we must intentionally sow seeds in our community to initiate change. She concluded that the seeds we sow now, good or bad, would eventually grow and we should want a good harvest.

Teens have a lot of energy bottled up inside. As the saying goes, "An idle mind is the devil's workshop." Placing them in environments where they can participate in volunteer and community services is an ideal way to redirect negative behavior and engage them in positive activities that are transferable as they move forward in society.

How Can I Serve You?

Integration of Social Media

Working with teens requires a great deal of patience and energy. Youth Leaders attempt to teach and train them during their formative years. This is critical to how they would go forth in life with an understanding of who Jesus Christ is and carry life lessons with them as they matriculate both academically and socially. Unfortunately, there may be times they do not seem to understand the purpose of a Youth Leader or the significance of their involvement. As they grow older, Youth Leaders are in great competition for sharing quality time with teens who frequently prefer to be on their cell phones and hang out with friends. In fact, a report from the Arizona University Information Technology Service, states that today's youth, referred to as Generation Z, or the iGeneration are interested in connections that are rapid and instantaneous, then removed as quickly as they existed. Technology is how they define themselves. The plethora of choices varies and may require investigating, such as the new app, Yellow, which was designed for ages 13 to 17. According to an NBC Today "Orange Room" segment, it enables teens to view profiles and swipe right or left much like the dating app, Tinder, if they identify someone they would like to meet in person; 96% of the parents surveyed found the app dangerous. There is also a fear of adult predators. The implication for us as Youth Leaders is that even when we think we have consistently done a good job engaging teens, we may not get the feedback that we expect. Recognizing these are our next generation of scientist, health providers, engineers, and perhaps teachers, we must continually be in prayer asking God to help us to learn how to appropriately incorporate new endeavors such as technology in our efforts to connect with youth. Teenagers are in their formative years. Along with the unpredictable influences of life, there are various pressures that mold and shape their personality. Regrettably, there are so many, naming them all would be close to impossible. Also, to talk about them in depth would be too lengthy, but to get the attention of those who are passionate about understanding the importance of technology to teens, the following should be noted. Our attention should be directed towards the positive. According to Ephesians 35:31, the skill that teens gain through the use of technology is a gift from God; however, it becomes our task as Youth Leaders to develop an interest through *gentleness* and care by learning to communicate with a technical vocabulary, research, take a class, offer a workshop, or schedule time to gain knowledge from teens so that we can become more technological astute. "For we (too) are His workmanship, created in Christ Jesus for good works, that God prepared beforehand so that we would walk in them," Ephesians 2:10. Youth Leaders should equip themselves to identify technological strategies that can be incorporated in teen meetings, or perhaps used as an icebreaker or activity. Also, meetings can be conducted with the use of power point presentations. Another example for using technology in a fun way is by applying Word Cloud creation tools such as ABCYa! TagCrowd, Tagul, Tagxedo, Tricklar, WordClouds, WorditOut, Wordle or another program that creatively groups words. With some assistance from an individual that is technologically savvy, allow teens to use their cell phones to respond to a series of five questions and project their response on a wall or screen. They will love to see how their ideas come together and can be viewed in an art form of a picture or collage.

Reflect and list some ways technology can creatively be used in sessions with teens:

_____

_____

How Can I Serve You?

Virginia S Rector, MCRP, MA, MTS

Questionnaire: How Are Teens Responding

On occasion, I have asked myself do teens understand ministry. Also, whether or not teens are connecting to the overall mission and purpose of ministries designed for them. Youth advisors commit time and effort to plan workshops and activities designed to meet teens where they are, but on the contrary, they are not sure if they are effective. In an effort to bridge the gap, the strategy used to assess this need was to create a questionnaire that would allow them to freely express their thoughts. The target group was a focus group of ten teens that included both boys and girls. The questions asked were as follows:

1.) What are you passionate about? What motivates you? What do like about church?
2.) What don't you like about church?
3.) What do you like to do in your free time?

4.) Where are you on social media; how do you hang-out? For example, snapchat, Instagram, YouTube, Facebook, other, please list.

5.) What do you want to be when you grow up?

6.) Is there a particular workshop or activity you would like to see addressed?

Once the questions were answered, the next step would be to determine how the church would respond. How would the church gain trust among youth and follow-through? What would the plan of action be to move to the next level? Responses by the teens were as follows:

1.) **What are you passionate about?**

Being successful in life and being close to God

"Acting" and church (two out of ten)

Playing soccer (two out of ten)

Painting

Reading and writing

Helping people

"I will soon be going to college"

Playing football, having a good time with my friends

Photography and culinary

"My family, my education, my future"

What motivates you?

"My mom and my family"

"The Word of God, wanting to have fun"

"Has to be something I like and enjoy"

"I like to create things and experiment a lot," "to try new things to see what (my project) will look like"

"I like to be active"

"My mom (three out of ten)"

"People in my family who help support me"

"One day, earning a lot of money and being successful"

"..., and my brothers"

"My grand mom and my friends who care about me"

How Can I Serve You?

What do you like about church?

"Learning more about God," "how I get a chance to interact with other kids," "everyone in the church is friendly, and no one is really mean"

"The songs that the choir sings and Pastor Rector's preaching, how to work with people my age and older people"

"How there are different activities for the youth, some churches don't have that, I like how they try to get us to participate and stuff"

"I like that there are a lot of different ministries to choose from, I like Sunday School and how they want us to learn more and different ways to interact, I like how they have workshops like the recent conflict thing so we will know how to deal with different situations"

"To hear the Word and activities"

"Meeting new people, and getting to know people better and you get to get more into the Word"

"Praise dance because it allows you to express yourself in different ways about God"

"The culture and the vibe (everyone is positive)"

"You can be yourself, we're all like one big family, we can go to each other if we need to talk or if we need anything"

"The way the Pastor preaches and makes it interesting and fun, the way everyone treats you like family"

2.) **What don't you like about church?**

"I can't think of anything that you guys have done"

"Sometimes the church is a little chilly (two out of ten)"

"There's really nothing I don't like about church (three out of ten)"

"Some people are so judgmental instead of trying to understand, they like to judge"

"The fake people, people are nice to you in church-they still talk about you behind your back" "Sometimes it (the worship service) goes so long on Sundays"

"We have to be there early in the mornings"

"There is nothing I don't like"

   3.) **What do you like to do in your free time**?

"I like to play football in my spare time, go to the movies, go out to eat and chill"

"I like to hang-out with my friends (four out of ten)"

"Going outside, going to the mall and shopping (three out of ten)"

"Read books that are in a series (I like to read each one to discover what will happen next)"

"I like to spend time with family (four out of ten)"

"Drawing, listening to music"

"Writing, reading and watching TV"

"Volleyball, mostly studying"

4.) **Where are you on social media; how do you hangout? For example, snapchat, Instagram, YouTube, Facebook, other, please list.**

"Texting and Instagram" (ten out of ten)

"Snapchat" (nine out of ten)

"YouTube" (three out of ten)

"Facebook" (two out of ten)

"Twitter" (four out of ten)

5.) **What do you want to be when you grow up?**

"A professional football player and physical therapist (two out of ten)"

"An actor or pediatric nurse"

"Forensic scientist"

"Fashion or interior designer"

"I want to work with kids"

"Architectural engineering"

"A midwife nurse"

"A chef and a photographer"

How Can I Serve You?

"A dentist and an anesthesiologist"

Interestingly, when teen girls begin with their youth ministry, they are 13 years old and in the 8th grade. By the time they are preparing to graduate from high school, they are 17 or 18 years old. It is amazing the influence God allowed us to have during a period of four or five years and the effect it could have on the teens we encountered just before entering adulthood. With prayer, the questionnaire mentioned earlier consisted of questions dear to the heart, addressed where teens were, as well as their future aspirations. Keeping in mind that in a few years, they would move from pre-millennial to millennial, questions one through four were the same and five and six focused on questions appropriate to ask the millennial Young Women's Ministry. These questions also allowed for comparison in maturation of responses.

They were:

1.) What are you passionate about?

"Helping people, having meaningful relationships with people"

"Being able to find self-love and self-confidence within"

"Health and that everyone has good health opportunities, youth are on the right path and that they always have someone they can go to, music"

"Right now, getting through school"

"Cooking"

How Can I Serve You?

What motivates you?

"My brother, I want to be a good role model for him and other young people and making sure I'm doing the right thing"

"My mother"

"Other people - older people are going into the same career field that I'm interested in" "Looking at the bigger picture of being a nurse, going to school and getting good grades - I motivate myself"

"My (2 yr. old) daughter"

2.) What do you like about church?

"The singing part of the church, singing is what I love to do, the musical side is spiritual for me the fellowship, how welcoming it is (two)"

"It is family oriented, (there is) something for any age to be involved with - it doesn't matter what background you come from, you don't have to have the same level of faith."

"I love the atmosphere, how everyone is family, if someone is down someone reaches out to you-someone will talk to you, I love the young women's ministry."

"I get to learn about the Bible and a lot of things like the different programs in the church like our Young Women's Ministry, and I like the Daughters In Christ."

3.) What don't you like about the church? Why or why not?

"Not many opportunities in the church for young people"

"It's a place you think you can come to and not be judged and oftentimes you are"

"Sometimes you feel like you have to act a certain way or behave a certain way when really you don't have to"

"Nothing I don't like about our family at our church"

"I wish that when the pastor is teaching us about the Bible he would break it down for our generation so we can understand."

4.) What do you like to do in your free time?

"Exercise"

"I write a lot and listen to music"

"Take naps, write, go out with friends a lot, eat"

"Catch-up on homework"

"Clean, read, take walks, drive, and cook"

5.) Where are you on social media?

"Instagram"(3)

"Snapchat"(4)

"Facebook"(4)

"Where I can express myself"

"YouTube"(3)

"LinkedIn"(2)

"Texting"

"Twitter"

"Netflix"

"I take a lot of pictures of my daughter"

6.) What do you want to do in a few years from now?

"(I'm) still trying to figure it out, I'm passionate about public health"

"Working in a practice as a physical therapist, returning to school, and eventually owning my own physical therapy practice"

"Working in some type of healthcare area, living in my own place, stronger in my faith than now, more educated"

"I want to be working in a hospital or in a doctor's office as a head nurse"

"I want to own my restaurant"

7.) What workshop topic(s) would you like to have discussed in your ministry?

"How to figure out life after college while in your 20's, reading the Bible, understanding it and having faith in God, (what do you do) when things don't go as planned"

How Can I Serve You?

"Something geared towards my age group; more activities - something that gives us a chance to open-up"

"Starting from teenhood to 30's how to keep your faith strong in education, work, friends, and family, how the insecurities and lack of faith in the future will get better, *hope*"

"(What is) the proper way to dress and become involved with dating a (godly) male" "Domestic violence, how would you identify a man of Christ that I should date?"

"I wish the pastor would break the Word down so, I can understand"

Reflect and list other questions or possible things that motivate youth.

_____

_____

_____

_____

How Can I Serve You?

Doing Something

How Will the Church Respond: How Can Ministries Collaborate?

Adult Leaders in the church shared that many of the responses provided on the questionnaire by the teens were things they once said when they were a teen themselves. They agreed the church must become proactive in addressing the concerns of teens, like providing Bibles that make sense to them as they read in order to understand the scriptures. For example, they talked about creating opportunities for teens to teach adults some of the various and unique operations of cell phones that young people have patience to learn on their own. Some new endeavors they mentioned were to allow teens, with some guidance to lead a workshop. They also discussed encouraging teens to bring their friends to weekly events like Sunday Church School and Bible Study. They thought that teens may find getting involved in more hands-on activities interesting; they added, this is a possibility that should be discussed with other ministry leaders. Church leaders are also willing to seek additional training and attend workshops that will help them to remain up-to-date while working with teens. The work of all church ministries may be compared to the work of teams in Nehemiah 3:1-32; working with youth is a team effort. In particular, involvement with youth requires a variety of attributes, which includes, but is not limited to energy, stamina, fortitude, patience, love, care, understanding, fairness, astuteness, tenacity, and synergy. At Pilgrim, there are several opportunities for Youth Leaders to collaborate with the Education Ministry, Junior Ushers, Young Warriors, Liturgical Dancers, Sewing Ministry, Technology Ministry, Audio, Sunday School Ministry, and Drama Ministry. Also, if other ministries are creative, countless ways can be developed for youth to experience intergenerational opportunities through volunteering and service learning. Some advantages of collaborating are that costs can be shared so ministries will not waste time duplicating efforts. Youth leaders, as well as other leaders should also come together to pray for strength, guidance and to remain focused so that their efforts will always be done to the Glory of God. In other words, do not exalt yourself, stay humble.

For millennials to accomplish their desire to have a free space to express themselves, encourage them to attend Young Adult Ministry meetings and incorporate a Bible Study, Sunday School with their peers, and plan a conference with qualified Christian workshop presenters who can address concerns that are unique to their generation; invite other age groups to attend.

Reflect and list various ways the youth you work with can collaborate with other ministries:

How Can I Serve You?

Youth Leaders wanting to contribute toward long-term success of teens believe there are things we can train teens to do. Also, we should share what we learn with others who have had experiences or expertise that can impact the lives of teens. I Peter 2:17 makes an eye-catching statement, "Honor the Emperor." If we believe, then we can teach leaders (i.e., pastors, teachers, adults) according to Romans 13:1, we learn to accept the good and disregard that which is not. Continual teaching and learning brings us all up-to-date and assists with keeping teens from feeling that we have 'stinking thinking' in our actions and beliefs. If you want to be respected, you must treat others with respect. Teach teens that I Peter 3:15-16 tells us we don't have to follow every trend that comes along. Whether by word or deed, they should have a Godly opinion and be prepared to give an answer at the appropriate moment; however, it may not be the opinion of the majority of their peers. Remind them that the enemy does not want them to focus on doing what is right.

Fashion, dress code for teens is oftentimes controversial among older generations. Both teen boys and girls should be concerned about demonstrating God's glory with their bodies (I Corinthians 6:19-20; Proverbs 7:10). They should be caring about the spiritual mindset of their brothers and sisters in Christ, Romans 15:1-2. As they select their clothing, they may think to themselves, "Am I wearing this outfit to catch the eye of someone I'd like to find me attractive, or I am wearing my outfit to look pleasant as I go my way?" Matthew 6:22 says, "The light of the body is the eye." Remind them that according to Proverbs 25:28, we cannot control the opinion of others, but we can control ourselves and our own intentions. While working in public education, I developed a mentoring relationship with a tenth-grade teen who had low self-esteem; she was full-figured and stood taller than most of her peers. Unfortunately, she had developed a reputation for being confrontational with teachers. As we walked together in the hallway, she asked me how I thought she looked; she was concerned about her personal image. My response to her was that, "You are beautiful because we are made in the image of God." She did not understand that we do not belong to the world, and we do not have to allow it to conform us into an image of whom or what the world thinks we should be. In our daily walk, too often we observe broken people and broken relationships. According to the scriptures, in Christ, we are a new creation, 2 Corinthians 5:17. With prayer, teens need to be taught that they were made in the image of a divine being higher than themselves. Learning to love oneself is a first step to learning how to develop a relationship with our Lord and Saviour Jesus Christ.

According to a message rendered by Pastor A.R. Bernard of the Christian Cultural Center, we must be mindful that when something good is taken away or absent from a person, satan looks for a void, a vacuum or an empty space to fill with evil. Being familiar with the scriptures, the Word, fills us with the Holy Spirit. In comparison to the student, he reiterated that "satan comes to steal our peace, courage, love, joy and relationship."

How Can I Serve You?

Formation and Transformation

As mentioned earlier, adolescence is a time when teens are formulating. They have a lot going on inside and out. They can transition from being very sociable to preferring to being isolated. This is a very emotional time for them. Therefore, it is imperative to listen to them with your heart. In today's world, oftentimes youth are sent to church as a relief to parents. In other words, parents may want a break from having to deal with the day-to-day challenges and stages that teens go through. The church is viewed as a place of relief, a safe place for teens to go. Furthermore, there are parents who want their teens to experience Christian formation. They desire to see a change, a difference that is positive, in their teen's behavior. Therefore, they expect the church to make it happen. As we continue to develop a relationship with parents, as well as encourage them to come to church with their child, we have a mandate with teens. While going through life's journey, Youth Leaders may be the first to introduce teens to prayer and how to look to Jesus Christ for strength. Youth Leaders are transformers. Our challenge is to guide them in a manner whereby they can reflect on circumstances that are beyond their control and begin to make space within to believe, as well as trust in a power higher than themselves. This effort brings about transformation and may also lead to them guiding their parent(s) to Christ. Teens are confronted daily by multiple conditions that often require making a quick decision. For example, while visiting a youth worship service, a teen shared an experience regarding a situation that occurred at school. She said she could have easily reacted in a negative manner, but instead quickly discerned that she had no control and concluded that all she could do was pray. Proverbs 17:28 teaches, "Even a fool, when he holdeth his peace, is counted wise: and he that shutteth his lips is esteemed a man (person) of understanding."

Teens should be encouraged to always communicate with God in prayer and set aside time to read the scriptures from a translation they can understand. If necessary, provide them with a Bible written on their level, easy to read, and understandable. Transformation involves having a nature that is conscionable not one that is unconscionable. While working weekends in security, John Cohn, II says that parents also seem to appreciate sending their youth to teen centers for 13-17-year-olds which, may accommodate as many as 330 in an evening. It serves as a means to keep them off the streets, supervised and in a safe collective location. On the other hand, there are teens from the moment they enter the facility who transform (behaviorally) into a different, unrecognizable person. The teens are in search of an evening with a false sense of fulfillment. Some become wild and free with minimal consequences. He believes that for them, it is the adventure of instant gratification that is appealing. He added that "blind conformity" happens almost instantaneously from the time they enter the door as they imitate, nice or not whatever their peer does. John says the behavior derives from them having too much freedom and desiring positive attention. While leading youth in the community, he suggests to stay prayed up, focus on the journey, not the struggle, dare to care, and know that teens are not the enemy, nor your equal; you are the trained, experienced adult.

We want teens to develop a loving and caring character, the earlier this is conveyed the better. In the New Testament of the Bible, teens can read about Jesus Christ, who at the age of twelve was a "sponge for knowledge." He learned and asked questions because of

How Can I Serve You?

His personal relationship with God so He could help others understand the relationship we can have with Him today. Through reading scriptures and talking to God, teens can come to the realization that there is no shame in focusing and practicing what is right.

Guidance in transformation often rest in the hands of parents and with Youth Leaders who assist with mentoring. Transformation requires a metamorphosis which involved navigating from one stage of development to the next; it is a renewing of the mind. Throughout their life, youth will experience one thing after another, but we don't want them to get stuck in a broken condition. Our faith in God must be passed along from generation to generation. We want to prepare caterpillars to become beautiful butterflies.

The summer before our son entered his senior year in high school, his cousin from Brooklyn, shared an opportunity for him to attend the Youth Theological Initiative at Emory University in Atlanta, a full-scholarship program sponsored by the Eli Lilly Foundation. The only problem was if he participated, he would miss the first week of high school football practice. A friend, from our hometown who was then Director of the YMCA Black Achievers Program, called and attempted to get our son to think about and prioritize the significance of this opportunity. Nevertheless, it was a quiet two-hour ride to Atlanta because he could not envision how he would benefit. However, our son had a life changing experience. Elizabeth Corrie, Director of the Youth Theological Initiative and Associate Professor in the Practice of Youth Education and Peacebuilding shares,

> "There appears to be no shortage of teenagers who want to be inspired and make the world better. But the version of Christianity

that some are taught doesn't inspire them 'to change anything that's broken in the world.' Teens want to be challenged; they want their tough questions taken on. We think that they want cake, but they actually want steak and potatoes, and we keep giving them cake. Churches, not just parents, share some of the blame for teens' religious apathy. ...The gospel of niceness can't teach teens how to confront tragedy. It can't bear the weight of deeper questions: Why are my parents getting a divorce? Why did my best friend commit suicide? Why, in this economy, can't I get the good job I was promised if I was a good kid?"

Encouraging teens to do what is right and oftentimes at best may require the use of some tough-love strategies. Kenda Creasy Dean, the Mary D. Synnott

Professor of Youth, Church, and Culture at Princeton Theological Seminary, during a lecture on youth leadership affirmed that teens prefer to be involved in ministry that has:

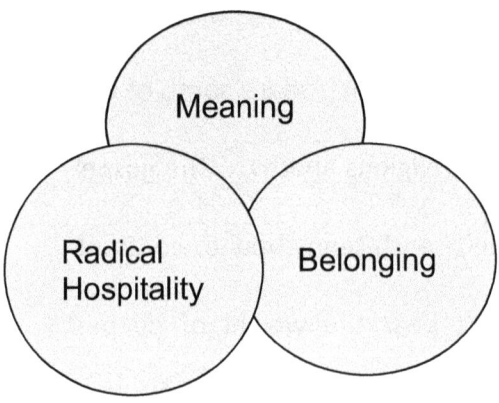

Teens want their church worship experience to have worth and magnitude, it must be *meaningful*. They want to feel welcomed and trust that they are genuinely wanted among the congregation-*radical hospitality*. They need to feel that they don't have to pretend, they want to be accepted for who they are, allow them to share their story, *belonging*. Rev. Dr. Otis Moss, III during the 2018 Dunkle-Mackey Seminar for Preachers intimated that rather than be told, humans want to be shown. He declared this occurs by demonstrating how to live (i.e., applying these attributes) which, is the best form of persuasion.

Community Partnerships

A needs assessment should be conducted to determine how the work of Youth Leaders can have the greatest impact with the teens being served. This can be done by conducting a focus group, teen interviews, survey, or questionnaire. Deep thought and meditation should be given to designing your questions to include the interest of teens, as well as things you need to know about them. From the assessment, you may be able to create a list of service learning and collaborative opportunities, as well as, a curriculum that can be used for training. The curriculum may be administered during monthly meetings and should incorporate information the teens provide to request guest speakers and prepare for interactive workshops. Also, it can address a combination of life skills and career goal setting strategies. Since teens enjoy spending their parent's money, you may choose to begin with a workshop on money management. Also, relationships with agencies, organizations, and businesses can be formed. For example, having over 10 years of experience as Director of Career Services helped with coordinating a Career Day for Youth specifically focusing on areas of interests shared from the career assessment. A Career Exploration event that covers a wider range of careers or a Career Fair combining the participation by both professionals and potential employers can also be planned. The larger the event, more partnerships should be formed and the greater the commitment for participation. As a Youth Leader, you will need to determine your strengths that work best, as well as collaborate with another entity or ministry to share the responsibility of organizing the event. When we are focused on the same mission, we should live out the words of I Thessalonians 5:11 to encourage each other and build one another up. For instance, the umbrella organization from which you are operating, or another organization that you collaborate with may be willing to use its tax ID number and letterhead to make a special appeal for donations. Also, do your homework to find sponsors and organizations with a passion for youth developing to their fullest potential. It may also be possible to partner with nonprofit organizations that have a similar mission and vision.

Virginia S Rector, MCRP, MA, MTS

Conclusion

Teenagers are in their formative years, remember, they are experiencing a series of emotions. They can vacillate from being sociable to not wanting to be bothered. Be on the alert for mood swings and behavioral shifts and not too quick to judge. They want someone to listen and understand them. Remember, words can be helpful or hurtful, so when in their presence always show compassion. From time-to-time share scriptural nuggets without being overbearing. Invest in their early years and provide some structure, it is often desired. In order to acquire their favor, display a nice personality and patience. Youth Leaders must be ready to meet teens where they are and identify values both parties have in common so that relationships can be formed. If possible, get their parents involved. Advocate for their community of faith to ensure that they are aware of the various ministries and resources that are available. Guide them on how to access them, this creates for them an environment that is nurturing. Teach them about Jesus Christ. Train them to read the scriptures and to love and care for others. Develop a budget as a resource for services, programs, and projects. When planning activities, include some of their suggestions; encourage their creativity, but present a limited amount of choices with guidance. Remember, wisdom has its place.

Offer opportunities for them to fellowship with their peers and participate in intergenerational ministry, which include all ages. This will help them to learn to respect and appreciate persons who are not like them. Also, collaborate with other ministries to participate in service learning and various developmental activities; you will find this to be cost effective. Become aware of cell phone apps that are popular and most preferred by youth, on the other hand, be alert that some may be dangerous. However, discover ways to appropriately incorporate technology within the ministry. Begin to pray corporately with other Youth Leaders and with the teens. Pray without ceasing and stand ready to be a peacemaker, the need may arrive unexpectedly. Prayer is the only way we can communicate with God, encourage it. Reflect on the praying mother or grandmother who prayed for you; prayers are still being lifted, they still work. God heard their prayers, He will hear yours. Occasionally, encourage teens by planning a recognition celebration, their self-image is being formed. Remember, it is important for them to have fond memories of the time you shared with them. There will be times they will recall, reflect and later return to their training to use as a tool to guide and pass along to other youth. Model behavior that you want to be adaptable to teens. Just in case the following were overlooked, please allow the Holy

How Can I Serve You?

Spirit to store in your heart "fresh fruit," which will flow through you. It is being shared below at a glance.

Love – "If I speak in the languages of humans and angels but have no love, I have become a reverberating gong or a clashing cymbal." *1 Corinthians 13:1*

Joy – "You make known to me the path of life; you will fill me with joy in your presence." *Psalms 16:11*

Peace – "Peace I leave with you; my peace I give to you. Not as the world gives do I give to you." *John 14:27*

Longsuffering – "And we know that all things work together for good to them that love God, to them who are the called according to [His] purpose." *Romans 8:28-29*

Kindness – "My little children, let us not love in word, neither in tongue; but indeed and in truth." *1 John 3:18*

Goodness – "[I had fainted], unless I had believed to see the goodness of the LORD in the land of the living." *Psalm 27:13*

Faithfulness – "He that is faithful in that which is least is faithful also in much:" Luke 16:10-12

Gentleness – "with all humility and gentleness, with patience, showing tolerance for one another in love," *Ephesians 4:2*

Self-Control – "For God gave us a spirit not of fear but of power and love and self-control." 2 *Timothy 1:7*

As youth leaders, these characteristics must continually be modeled with compassion.

How Can I Serve You?

Epilogue

You may ask yourself the question, when will I know that I have found my true calling, am I a Youth Leader? When without much effort, you read articles or find yourself listening to information about youth whether on the Internet, T.V, radio or through conversations and it becomes an attention grabber, jot down those things that are of interest in a journal. Pray and ask God, in the name of Jesus, how you can make a difference. When you prefer to do activities with youth and find they enjoy being with you, have a little talk with Jesus about the gifts he has bestowed and how you may effectively use them. When you feel that you share conversations that can pour something positive into a teen's life, ask God to continue to bless you to bless them. When you have a burning desire to advocate for teens, teen issues, support programs and attend workshops that are teen oriented, or perform tasks that will add to their quality of life, ask the Lord is this what you want me to do? Also, when you pray more for youth than you pray for yourself, pray to God for the direction he wants you to pursue. Listen for His voice; God will answer your prayer. Bishop Barbara Amos, a renown community builder affirms that "all members (including youth leaders) are unique, meaningful, and purposeful to the accomplishment of God's purpose."

As you collaborate, understand that community is built inside and outside of the church. "Finally, my brothers and sisters, whatever is true, whatever is noble, whatever is right, whatever is pure, whatever is lovely, whatever is admirable—if anything is excellent or praiseworthy—think about such things. Whatever you have learned or received or heard from me or seen in me—put it into practice. And the God of peace will be with you, Amen." Philippians 4:8-9

References

Centers for Disease Control and Prevention, About Teen Pregnancy. (2017, May 9). Reproductive Health: Teen Pregnancy:

https://www.cdc.gov/teenpregnancy/about/index.htm

Erickson, T. (2012, April). *General Issues: How Mobile Technologies Are Shaping A New Generation.* Harvard Business Review. https//hbr.org/2012/04/themobile-re-generation

Esposito, L. (2015, November 11). *When Kids Are the Caregivers*. U.S. News and World Report.

https://www.health.usnews.com/health-news/patient-advice/articles/2015/11/11/when-kids-are-the-caregivers

Horn, B. Parra, E. Jedra, C. Reyes, J. Fenn, L. (2017, September). Wilmington: Most Dangerous Place In America for Youth. *Delaware News Journal.*

https://www.delawareonline.com/story/news/crime/2017/09/08/our-babies-killing-each-other/100135370/

Learning to Read, Reading to Learn: Early Warning! Why Reading by the End of Third Grade? Matters. A Kids Count Special Report from the Annie E. Casey Foundation. (2010). http://www.ccf.ny.gov/files/9013/8262/2751/AECFRepor-ReadingGrad3.pdf

How Can I Serve You?

McNeeley, C. Blanchard, J. (2009). *The Teen Years Explained: A Guide to Healthy Adolescent Development.*

https://www.jhsph.edu/research/centers-andinstitutes/center-for-adolescenthealth/_docs/TTYE-Guide.pdf

Richards-Gustafson, F. (2017, June). *The Effects of Bad Parenting On Children*.

http://www.livestrong.com/article/560572-the-effects-of-bad-parenting-on-children/

The Annie E. Casey Foundation's Kids Count Project. (2018, June). State Trends in Child Well-Being.

www.aecf.org/m/resources/aecf-2018 kidscountdatabook-2018.pdf

Wallace, K. (2016, July). *Half of Teens Think That They're Addicted to Their Smartphones.*

http://www.cnn.com/2016/05/03/health/teens-cell-phone-addictionparents/

Young, A. M, Cranford, S.E., Ross - Durow, P.L., Boyd, C. J. (2012, October 31). *Nonmedical Use of Prescription Opioids Among Adolescents: Subtypes Based On Motivation for Use. Journal of Addictive Disease.*

http://www.ncbi.nlm.nih.gov/pmc//articles/PMC3531808/

Youth on their Own: Supporting the High School Graduation and Continued Success of Homeless Youth.

http://yoto.org/about-us

Teen "Icebreakers" and Activities

Teen years, adolescence, is a formative age; teens are dealing with gender identification and building self-esteem.

Finding My Purpose and Destiny

Galatians 5:22-23 But the **fruit of the Spirit** is love, joy, peace, forbearance, kindness, goodness, faithfulness, gentleness and self-control.

Pick a fruit that would most likely be like you? In a few sentences, describe things you and the fruit have in common.

_____

_____

_____

_____

_____

_____

_____

_____

_____

_____

_____

_____

_____

_____

_____

_____

How do teens express themselves to others when they don't want to talk or be bothered? They are feeling anti-social, desiring isolation, perhaps even rejected.

How Can I Serve You?

What Makes Me Happy?

Proverbs 15:13, NIV A happy heart makes the face cheerful, but heartache crushes the spirit.

Proverbs 17:22, ESV A joyful heart is good medicine, but a crushed spirit dries up the bones.

Draw three emojis that describe when you are happy and give someone else a chance to describe your drawings. (Note: While the teens are drawing, consider playing a song like Kirk Franklin's "Do You Want to Be Happy," or "Smile")

Working with teens requires a great deal of patience and energy. This is critical to how they would go forth in life with an understanding of who Jesus Christ is and carry life lessons with them as they matriculate both academically and socially.

What do you enjoy doing when you have time alone?

Being Alone With God Is A Good Thing; Be Sure You Are Spending Some Time with HIM!

Matthew 6:6 But when you pray, go into your room, close the door and pray to your Father, who is unseen. Then your Father, who sees what is done in secret, will reward you.

Your friend's mom confidently shares with you that she is concerned because her teen is talking less and seemingly becoming more isolated in his or her bedroom. The teen has provided you with some detail that doesn't seem harmful.

Write down a text message prayer you would send to your friend to encourage him or her. (Consider playing "Hang On" by Kierra Sheard)

_____

_____

_____

_____

_____

Challenging Myself, Setting New Goals: Doing Something Different

Sunday Church School has teachers for each age level to help you to understand the Word of God. **Proverbs 3:16 (NIV)** Long life is in her right hand; in her left hand are riches and honor.

Proverbs 3:1-6 (NIV) My Son (daughter) forget not my law, but keep my commandments for length of days, long life and peace shall I add to thee.

*So, if God promises that I can live a longer, healthier life by learning the scriptures, what are **five** steps I can take to attend Sunday Church School at least once a month?*

1.) _____

_____

2.) _____

_____

3.) _____

_____

4.) _____

_____

5.) _____

_____

Our challenge is to guide teens in a manner whereby they can reflect on circumstances that are beyond their control and begin to make space within to believe, and trust in a power higher than them.

How Can I Serve You?

Out Of My Hands

Psalms 23: 1 "The Lord is my shepherd, I shall not want."

Psalms 91:4 (KJV) "He shall cover thee with his feathers, and under His wings shalt thou trust: His truth *shall be thy* shield and buckler."

Psalms 55:22 "Cast your cares on the Lord and He will sustain you; He will never let the righteous fall."

Take a look at the following scenario:

You and your best friend earn good grades and hate missing days from school. In fact, the two of you look forward to socializing at school. Your best friend was in the restroom when two other students entered. Your friend forgot that she left her cell phone on the sink. When she returned to get her cell phone, it was missing. Your friend questioned the girls about her cell phone. One of the girls replied, "I saw a message on your phone and you were talking about me." The two girls began to push your friend and an Assistant Principal walked in. Your friend told you that she did not participate in the pushing. Parents were called and the two girls, along with your friend, were expelled from school for two days. The decision was final.

How can you help your best friend? What will you be able to do? In a few sentences, share how you would respond. (Softly, consider playing Erica Campbell's song, "I Luh God")

_____

_____

_____

_____

_____

_____

Distractions will come, but how teens respond can often determine the outcome. Teens should be allowed to mature while participating in activities that are healthy and age-appropriate. As youth leaders we strive to help teens to develop a healthy and spiritual way of thinking which is grounded in the scripture, Proverbs 4:23 advises, "Above everything else, guard your heart for everything you do flows from it."

How Can I Serve You?

Peers Acting Like Alligators

Psalm 118:6-7 (ESV) The LORD is on my side; I will not fear. What can man do to me? The Lord is on my side as my helper; I shall look in triumph on those who hate me.

A new girl just transferred to your school. You are a nice person and the two of you have some things in common. She finds it easy to talk to you, but she is not sure how she should go about making new friends or trusting people. She doesn't like confusion and doesn't want to be taken advantage of. Since you can't always be with her, please give her some advice on how she should choose girls to hang with.

A.)

B.)

C.)

<u>D.)</u>

*When should she look for a warning signal that a person can be "bad news?"

What are some other suggestions you have to pass along to her regarding staying away from trouble?

"Children (*teens*) must have at least one person who believes in them. It could be a counselor, a teacher, a preacher, a friend. It could be you. You never know when a little love, a little support will plant a small seed of hope." Marian Wright Edelman

How Can I Serve You?

Believe it or not, Adults can learn some valuable lessons from you

Ephesians 4:26(NIV) "In your anger do not sin" (don't become revengeful): Do not let the sun go down while you are angry

When you get angry, what do you do? How do you handle your anger? When is the last time you participated in a caring and loving activity?

There are lots of adults who own cell phones, but don't know enough about how to use them; they simply don't get their money's worth like you do. If you were asked to teach a few adults about some of the special things that cell phones can do (i.e., block unwanted telephone numbers), what are some "need-to-know" things you would teach them?

I would teach them about_____

_____

I would show them how to_____

_____

Another thing they should know is_____

_____

I was surprised to find out that most adults don't know

how to_____

_____

_____

Notes

www.ingramcontent.com/pod-product-compliance
Lightning Source LLC
Chambersburg PA
CBHW071215160426
43196CB00012B/2311